Hip-hop Grooves for Bass

by Max Palermo

ISBN 13: 978-1-57424-225-6
ISBN 10: 1-57424-225-3

Copyright © 2007 CENTERSTREAM Publishing, LLC
P.O. Box 17878 - Anaheim Hills, CA 92817

All rights for publication and distribution are reserved.
No part of this book may be reproduced in any form or by any Electronic or mechanical means including information storage and
retrieval systems without permission in writing from the publisher, except by reviewers who may quote brief passages in review.

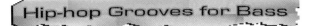

HIP-HOP: The History

Hip-hop music originated in the early 1970's in the South Bronx as a mix of funk, soul and R&B. The godfather was Kool DJ Herc, a Jamaican DJ who moved from Kingston to New York City in 1967. Here, he started to introduce the Jamaican style of improvising rhymes over the dub versions of reggae records. Herc's musical parties eventually gained notoriety. As he progressed, he adapted his style by cutting and mixing the instrumental versions of rare-groove classics for the MCs to rhyming in sync with the beats. Other big hip-hop pioneers as Afrika Bambaataa and Grandmaster Flash began to give their own performances, adding new mixing techniques and progressively inserting other sound solutions like rock music into the standard funk and disco playlists of the time.

Hip-hop quickly became a cultural movement within the urban Afro American and Puerto Rican youth, involving several forms of expression as DJing (cutting and scratching), MCing (rapping), graffiti art and break dancing.

In the early 1980's, small and independent record labels produced the first hip-hop records marketed almost exclusively to a black audience. The mainstream of the American music industry will be joined only in the middle of the decade, when white musicians too will embrace the new style. In 1986 hip-hop reached the top ten on the pop charts with the Beastie Boys and Run-DMC. In the same years the first female group, Salt-N-Pepa, broke into the scene.

In the 1990's hip-hop became more and more eclectic as many artists began to experiment with any sound source as folk music, be bop, and television news. In the UK, Tricky and Massive Attack invented a new genre called trip-hop by mixing jazz and hip-hop.

During the late 1990's and the 2000's, hip-hop went on to explode as an international phenomenon and became the mainstream itself. Now a multimillion-dollar industry dominates record sales worldwide, with widespread use of hip-hop music and images in everything from fashion and advertising to literature and film.

Within the past 20 years, many artists have greatly influenced the hip-hop scene: Public Enemy, 2Pac, Ice Cube, Cypress Hill, Missy Elliot, Eminem, 50 Cent, Nelly, Outkast, and Jay-Z to name a few.

This is just a brief history of a grassroots cultural movement spanning race and gender, language and nationality, and more than 30 years of creative contributions in music, dance, art and poetry. Reasons why hip-hop continues to be so popular today are the same as the early days. It offers urban youth a chance to freely express how they feel with the unique set rule to be original. Hip-hop is a lifestyle with its own language, style of dress, music and mind set that is continuously evolving. Hip-hop is made from whatever sound gives the right feel or groove: Latin, rock, disco, jazz, reggae, pop, techno, African, Arabic ... and definitely funk, soul and R&B.

About This Book

From the irresistible party jams of South Bronx to the urban sounds of today, hip-hop has maintained close links with the roots. Many of its characteristic sounds and beats come from funk, soul and R&B origins.

The electric bass does so play a key role in creating such groovin' which gives hip-hop a unique attractive feel.

This Book/CD set contains 90 authentic hip-hop licks that will lead you to the vibrant world of hip-hop style. All the bass lines are demonstrated on the CD's full-performance tracks and transcribed in standard notation and tablature.

Jamming along these patterns you will improve your technique while learning to lay down the right groove. Just listen to the tracks and concentrate on playing with a good time feel.

Enjoy!

About The Author

Bassist and educator living in Italy, Max Palermo has had extensive experience performing in show bands, concerts, club dates in the jazz, pop and funk worlds. He has toured with a number of artists in Italy and abroad, doing their television promotions and studio recordings for Sony, Polygram, and Cecchi Gori.

In addition to his career as a bass player, Max has been active as a bass instructor for over eighteen years, teaching in renowned music schools based in Genoa (Music Line) and Milan (C.P.M. and M.A.S.), and he is currently devoting himself to his writing and music training research activities.

Besides Hip-hop Grooves for Bass, he is the author of several bass instructional and reference books.

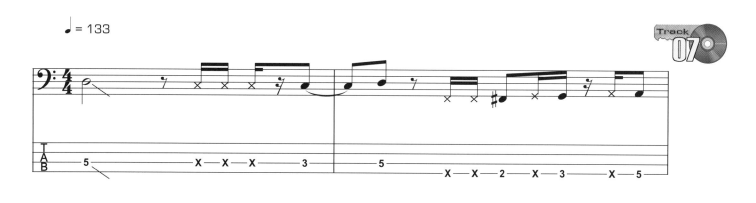

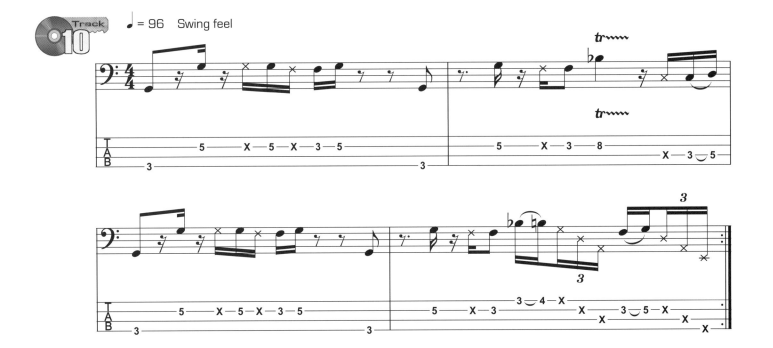

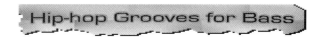

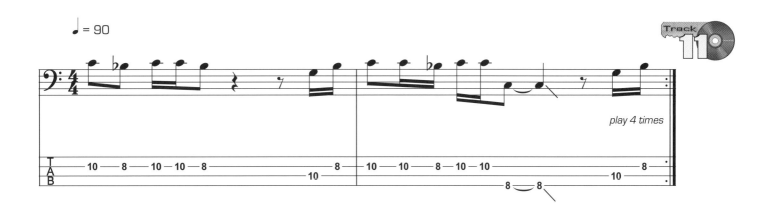

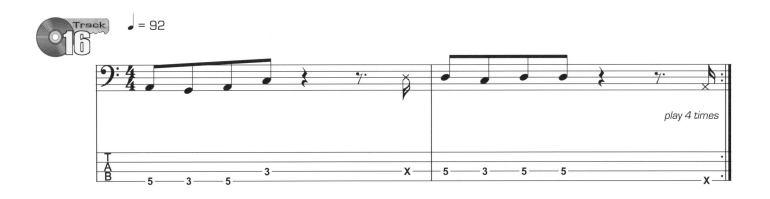

9

10

11

Track 28 ♩ = 98

play 4 times

Track 29 ♩ = 96

play 4 times

Track 30 ♩ = 134

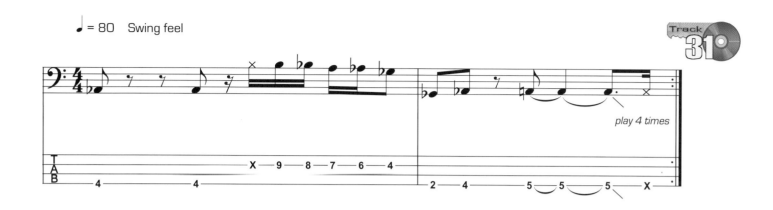

Track
35
♩ = 96   Swing feel

play 4 times

Track
36
♩ = 82

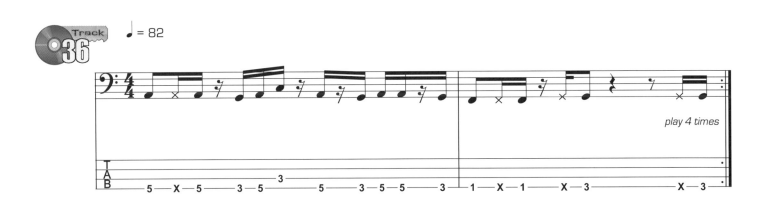

play 4 times

Track
37
♩ = 101

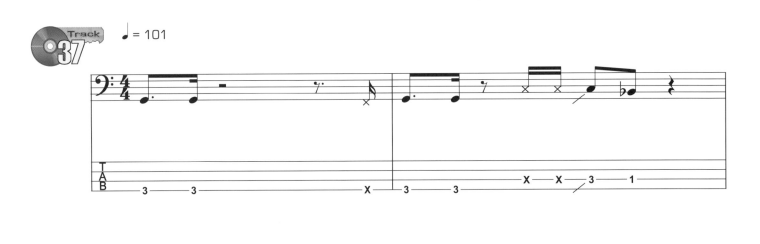

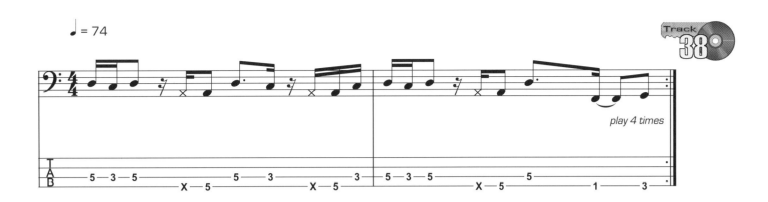

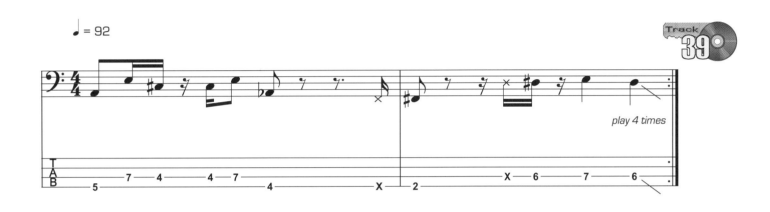

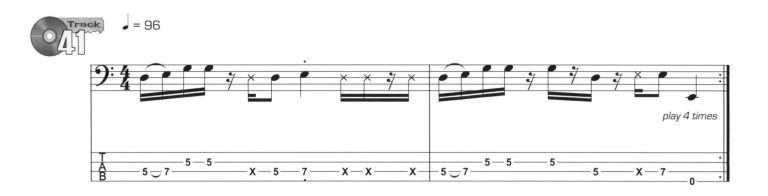

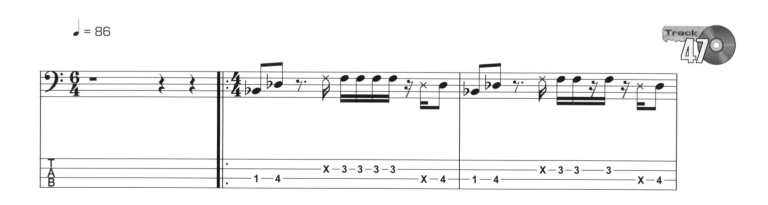

Track 48 ♩ = 82

play 4 times

Track 49 ♩ = 92

play 4 times

Track 50 ♩ = 96   Swing feel

play 3 times

Track 51 ♩ = 98

play 4 times

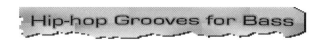

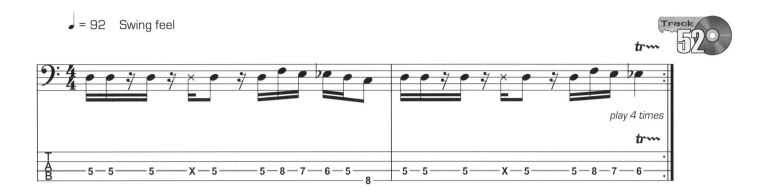

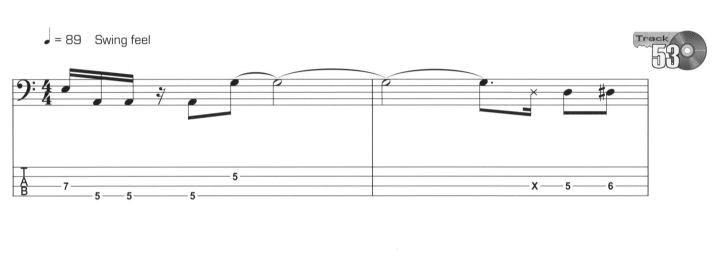

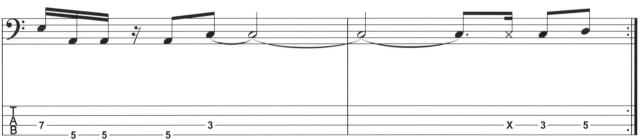

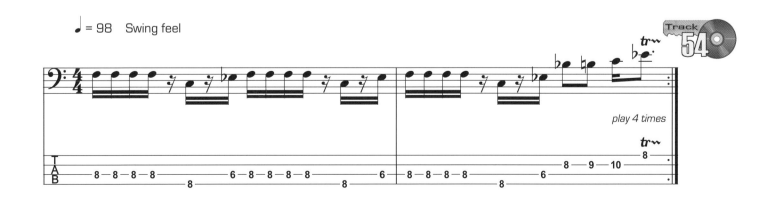

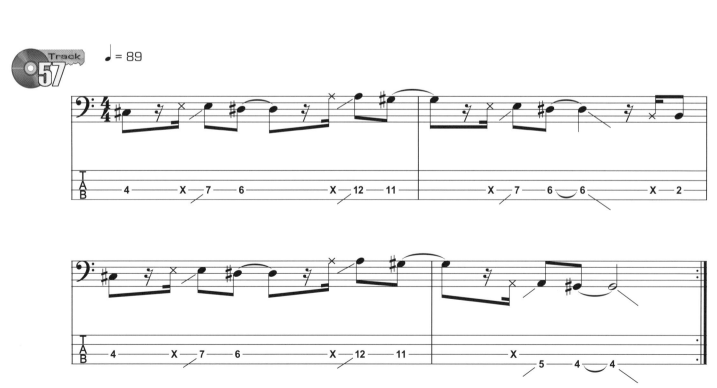

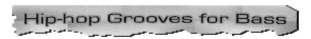

♩ = 89

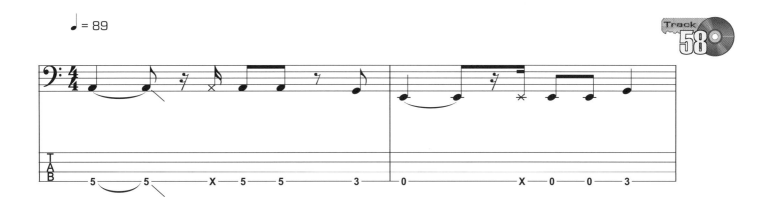

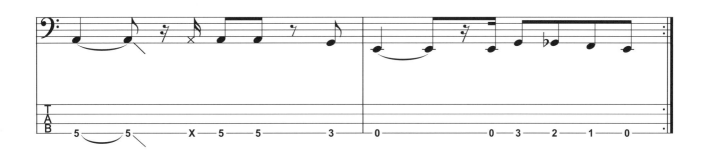

♩ = 96

play 4 times

♩ = 100

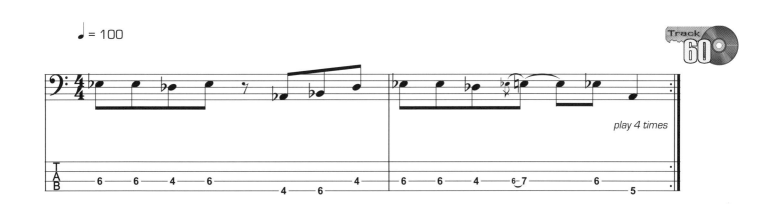

play 4 times

Track **61** ♩ = 90

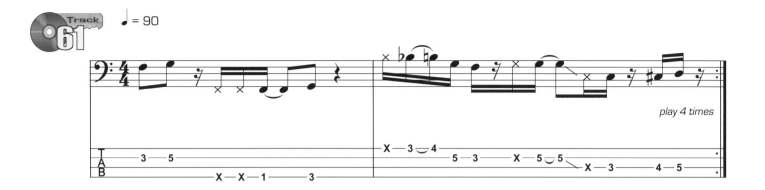

Track **62** ♩ = 100

Track **63** ♩ = 80   Swing feel

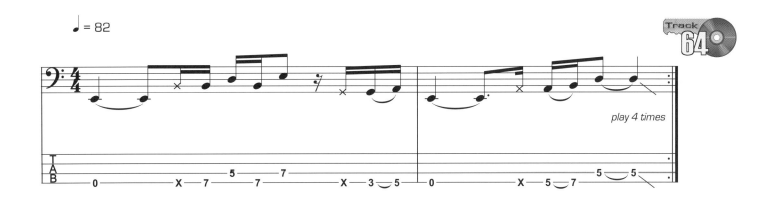

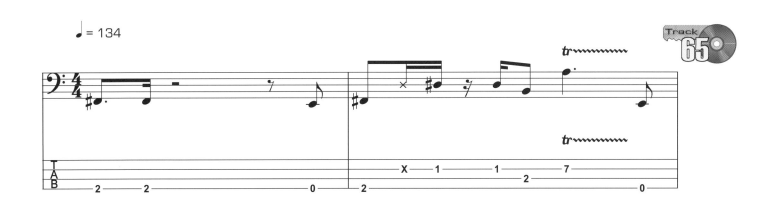

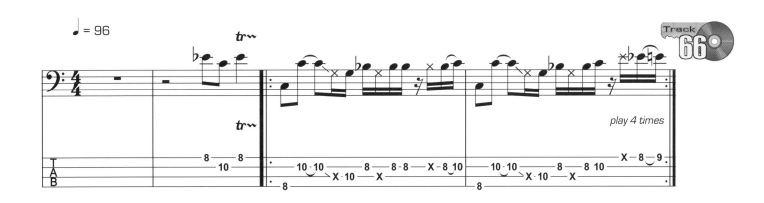

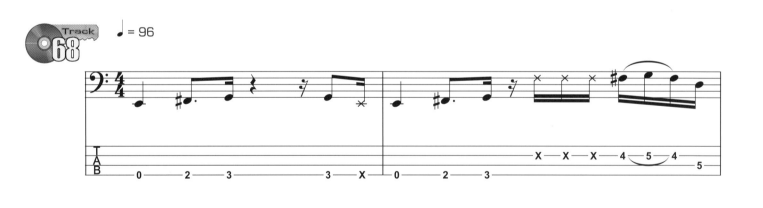

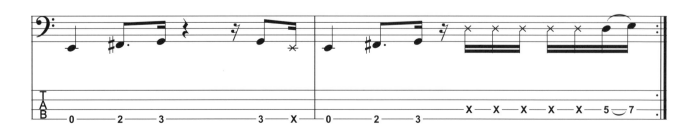

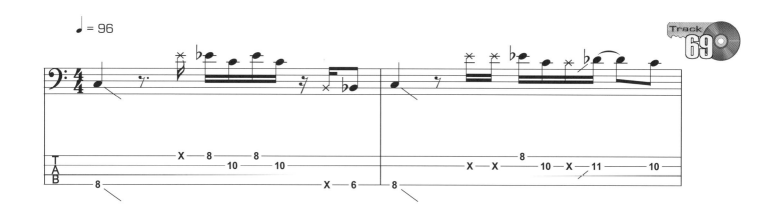

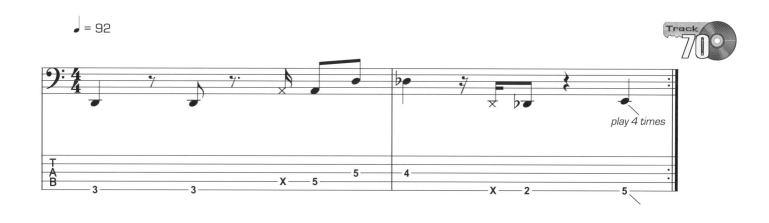

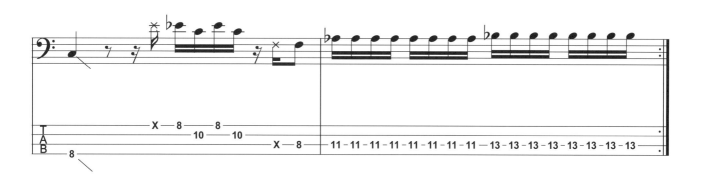

Track **72** ♩ = 82

play 4 times

Track **73** ♩ = 98

Track **74** ♩ = 101

play 4 times

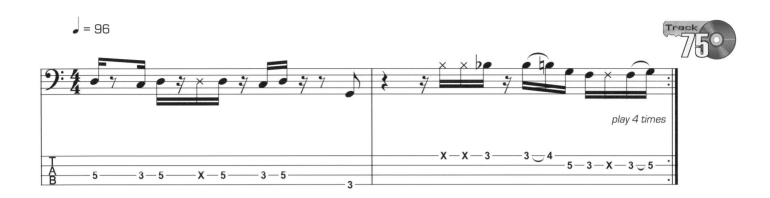

27

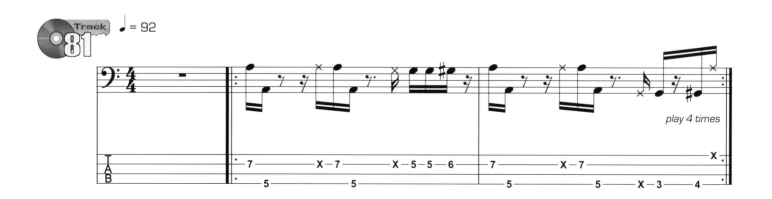

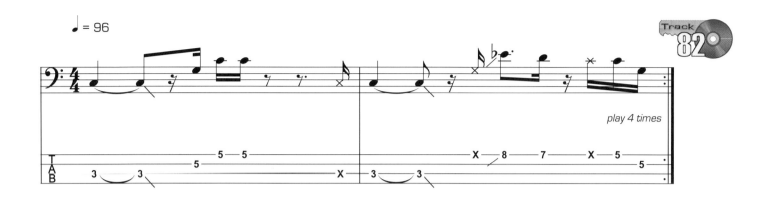

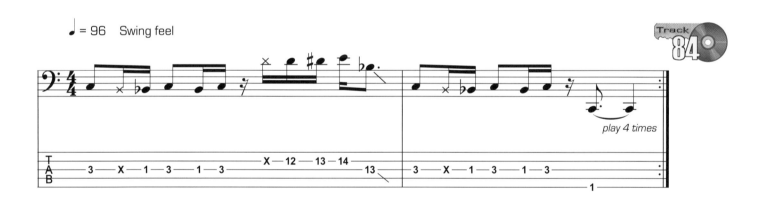

29

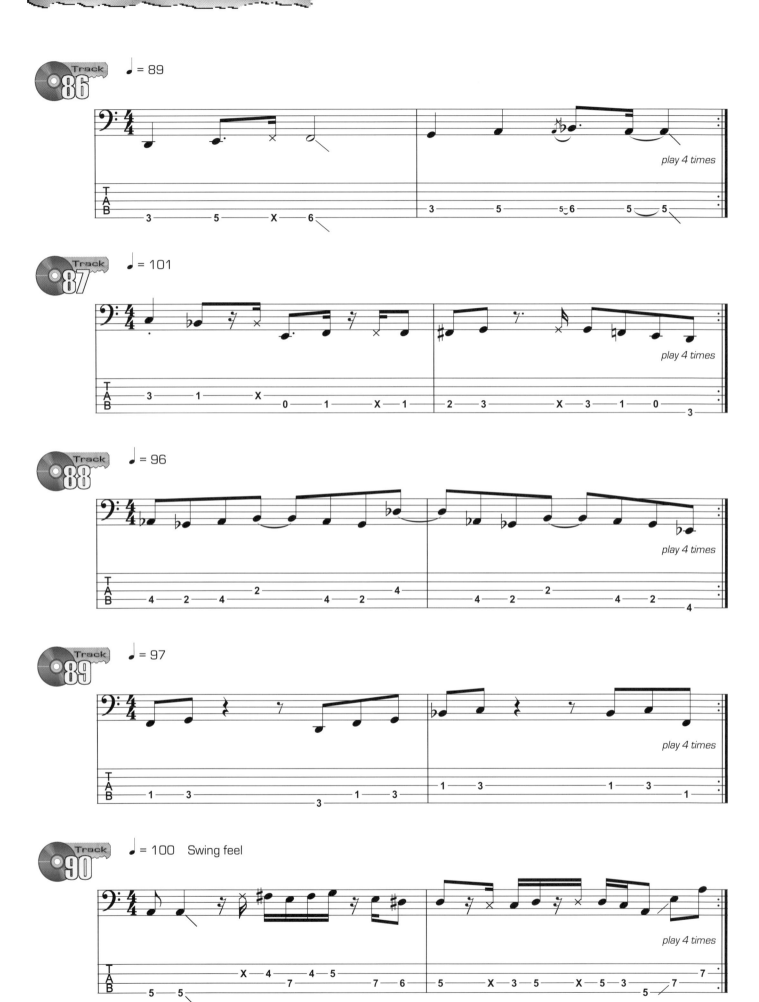

More Great Bass Books from Max Palermo...

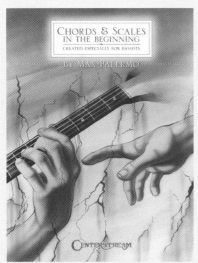

CHORDS & SCALES IN THE BEGINNING – CREATED ESPECIALLY FOR BASSISTS

by Max Palermo

A practical approach for playing scales over any chord progression to strengthen your bass lines, groove patterns and solo ideas. For 4 & 5 strings.

00001140 ....$14.95

ULTIMATE BASS EXERCISES

by Max Palermo

Bassist and educator living in Italy, Max Palermo has had extensive experience performing in show bands, concerts, club dates in the jazz, pop and funk worlds. He has toured with a number of artists in Italy and abroad, doing their television promotions and studio recordings for Sony, Polygram, and Cecchi Gori.

In addition to his career as a bass player, Max has been active as a bass instructor for over eighteen years, teaching in renowned music schools based in Genoa (Music Line) and Milan (C.P.M. and M.A.S.), and he is currently devoting himself to his writing and music training research activities.

Besides Ultimate Bass Exercises - Workbooks 1 & 2, he is the author of several bass instructional and reference books. 158 pages.

00000476..$19.95

P.O. Box 17878 - Anaheim Hills, CA 92817

(714) 779-9390   www.centerstream-usa.com

More Great Bass Books from Centerstream...

 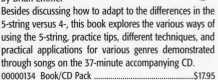

5-STRING BASS METHOD
by Brian Emmel

Besides discussing how to adapt to the differences in the 5-string versus 4-, this book explores the various ways of using the 5-string, practice tips, different techniques, and practical applications for various genres demonstrated through songs on the 37-minute accompanying CD.

00000134 Book/CD Pack $17.95

ART OF THE SLAP
by Brian Emmel

This slap bass method book, designed for advanced beginning to intermediate bassists, is based on the understanding and application of modes. The focus is on the concept of groove sculpting from modes, and not on actual right- and left-hand techniques. The CD features recordings of all the examples, plus a split-channel option to let you practice your playing. Includes 13 songs.

00000229 Book/CD Pack..................................$16.95

BASS GUITAR CHORDS
by Ron Middlebrook

84 of the most popular chords for bass guitar. Covers: finger placement, note construction, chromatic charts, and the most commonly used bass scales. Also has a helpful explanation of the common 2-5-1 progression, and the chords in all keys.

00000073 ....$2.95

BEGINNING TO ADVANCED 4-STRING BASS
by Brian Emmel

This instructional video by noted instructor/author Brian Emmel leaves no stone unturned in explaining all there is to know about 4-string bass basics! Designed for the beginning to advanced player, Brian's step-by-step demonstrations form the foundation for understanding music theory and building bass technique. Topics covered range from common musical terminology, to playing in a garage band, to laying down tracks in a recording studio. 60 minutes.

00000374 DVD $19.95

BLUES GROOVES
Traditional Concepts for Playing 4 & 5 String Blues Bass
by Brian Emmel

This book/CD pack has been designed to educate bass enthusiasts about the development of different styles and traditions throughout the history of the blues, from the 1920s to the early 1970s. Players will learn blues scales, rhythm variations, turnarounds, endings and grooves, and styles such as Chicago blues, jazz, Texas blues, rockabilly, R&B and more. The CD includes 36 helpful example tracks.

00000269 Book/CD Pack...............................$17.95

PURRFECT 4-STRING BASS METHOD
by Brian Emmel

This book will teach students how to sight read and to acquire a musical vocabulary. Includes progressive exercises on rhythm notation, 1st to 4th string studies, enharmonic studies, chords and arpeggios, blues progressions, and chord charts.

00000201 ....$9.95

ULTIMATE BASS EXERCISES
by Max Palermo

Bassist and educator Max Palermo takes you through more than 700 easy, step-by-step exercises for finger building, based on the 24 possible fingering combinations. 158 pages.

00000476 ....$19.95

P.O. Box 17878 - Anaheim Hills, CA 92817
(714) 779-9390   www.centerstream-usa.com